Chargebacks

Chargebacks

Chargebacks911 Special Edition

by Monica Eaton-Cardone

Chargebacks For Dummies®, Chargebacks911 Special Edition

Published by
John Wiley & Sons, Inc.
111 River St.
Hoboken, NJ 07030-5774
www.wiley.com

Copyright © 2018 by John Wiley & Sons, Inc., Hoboken, New Jersey

No part of this publication may be reproduced, stored in a retrieval system or transmitted in any form or by any means, electronic, mechanical, photocopying, recording, scanning or otherwise, except as permitted under Sections 107 or 108 of the 1976 United States Copyright Act, without the prior written permission of the Publisher. Requests to the Publisher for permission should be addressed to the Permissions Department, John Wiley & Sons, Inc., 111 River Street, Hoboken, NJ 07030, (201) 748-6011, fax (201) 748-6008, or online at http://www.wiley.com/go/permissions.

Trademarks: Wiley, For Dummies, the Dummies Man logo, Dummies.com, and related trade dress are trademarks or registered trademarks of John Wiley & Sons, Inc. and/or its affiliates in the United States and other countries, and may not be used without written permission. Chargebacks911 and the Chargebacks911 logo are trademarks or registered trademarks of Chargebacks911. All other trademarks are the property of their respective owners. John Wiley & Sons, Inc., is not associated with any product or vendor mentioned in this book.

LIMIT OF LIABILITY/DISCLAIMER OF WARRANTY: THE PUBLISHER AND THE AUTHOR MAKE NO REPRESENTATIONS OR WARRANTIES WITH RESPECT TO THE ACCURACY OR COMPLETENESS OF THE CONTENTS OF THIS WORK AND SPECIFICALLY DISCLAIM ALL WARRANTIES, INCLUDING WITHOUT LIMITATION WARRANTIES OF FITNESS FOR A PARTICULAR PURPOSE. NO WARRANTY MAY BE CREATED OR EXTENDED BY SALES OR PROMOTIONAL MATERIALS. THE ADVICE AND STRATEGIES CONTAINED HEREIN MAY NOT BE SUITABLE FOR EVERY SITUATION. THIS WORK IS SOLD WITH THE UNDERSTANDING THAT THE PUBLISHER IS NOT ENGAGED IN RENDERING LEGAL, ACCOUNTING, OR OTHER PROFESSIONAL SERVICES. IF PROFESSIONAL ASSISTANCE IS REQUIRED, THE SERVICES OF A COMPETENT PROFESSIONAL PERSON SHOULD BE SOUGHT. NEITHER THE PUBLISHER NOR THE AUTHOR SHALL BE LIABLE FOR DAMAGES ARISING HEREFROM. THE FACT THAT AN ORGANIZATION OR WEBSITE IS REFERRED TO IN THIS WORK AS A CITATION AND/OR A POTENTIAL SOURCE OF FURTHER INFORMATION DOES NOT MEAN THAT THE AUTHOR OR THE PUBLISHER ENDORSES THE INFORMATION THE ORGANIZATION OR WEBSITE MAY PROVIDE OR RECOMMENDATIONS IT MAY MAKE. FURTHER, READERS SHOULD BE AWARE THAT INTERNET WEBSITES LISTED IN THIS WORK MAY HAVE CHANGED OR DISAPPEARED BETWEEN WHEN THIS WORK WAS WRITTEN AND WHEN IT IS READ.

For general information on our other products and services, or how to create a custom *For Dummies* book for your business or organization, please contact our Business Development Department in the U.S. at 877-409-4177, contact info@dummies.biz, or visit www.wiley.com/go/custompub. For information about licensing the *For Dummies* brand for products or services, contact BrandedRights&Licenses@Wiley.com.

ISBN 978-1-119-51271-4 (pbk)

Manufactured in the United States of America

V090123_060418

Publisher's Acknowledgments

We're proud of this book and of the people who worked on it. Some of the people who helped bring this book to market include the following:

Development Editor: Steve Kaelble

Project Editor: Martin V. Minner

Editorial Manager: Rev Mengle

Senior Acquisitions Editor: Amy Fandrei

Business Development Representative: Ashley Barth

Production Editor: Siddique Shaik

Table of Contents

INTRODUCTION 1
    About This Book 1
    Foolish Assumptions 2
    Icons Used in This Book 2

CHAPTER 1: What's a Chargeback? 3
    Defining Chargebacks 3
    Understanding How Chargebacks Came into Existence 4
    How Chargebacks Happen Now 6
    Who's Involved in the Chargeback Process? 6

CHAPTER 2: The Chargeback Process 9
    The Initial Claim 9
    The Transfer of Funds 11
    The Dispute 12
    The Final Decision 13
    Time Is of the Essence 14

CHAPTER 3: Why Chargebacks Happen 15
    Reason 1: Criminal Fraud 15
    Even More Common: Merchant Error 17
    The Biggest Reason: Friendly Fraud 18
    Fraudsters Are Taking a Risk 20

CHAPTER 4: How Chargebacks Hurt Merchants 21
    Chargebacks Cost a Lot 21
    Chargebacks Threaten Your Lifeblood 22
    Chargebacks Can Look Bad 23

CHAPTER 5: Why the Chargeback Battle Is So Difficult 25
    Chargebacks Are Confusing 25
    The Playing Field Is Not Level 26
    Chances for Fraud Are Growing 27
    Unhappy Holidays 28

CHAPTER 6: **The Merchants Strike Back** 29

    Preventing Chargebacks 29
        Verifying the buyer 30
        Satisfying the customer 30
        Making billing clear 30
        Staying connected 31
        Being responsive 31
        Creating better processes 32
    Disputing Chargebacks 32
    Disputing Effectively 33
    Seeking Expert Help 34

CHAPTER 7: **Ten Essential Tips for Preventing Chargebacks** 35

    Connect with Customers 35
    To Err Is Dangerous 35
    Keep Tabs on Recurring Payments 36
    Ship Away Those Shipping Problems 36
    Honesty Is the Best Policy 36
    Check Your Toolkit 37
    Signs of Fraud 37
    Keep Your Data Secure 38
    More Friendly Fraud Prevention 38
    Talk to the Experts 38

APPENDIX: CHARGEBACK REASON CODES 39

Introduction

You've grown a business, made lots of excellent decisions, and the transactions are coming through faster and faster. It's invigorating! Just when you think you've won, someone snatches defeat from the jaws of your victory. That's what a chargeback feels like, and it isn't a good feeling.

Chargebacks happen when customers, for one reason or another, ask to get back the money that flowed from their charge card to your bank account. Only they didn't ask you, they asked the bank that issued the card, and one day the money you thought you earned vanishes from your account.

Besides being frustrating, chargebacks can wreak havoc on your cash flow and profitability. Even worse, if chargebacks happen too often, your card-processing fees can skyrocket, or you might even lose the privilege of taking plastic for payment at all. That's seriously bad news.

You don't have to sit back and take it, however. You need to implement a comprehensive chargeback strategy, and it must help you do two distinct things:

- Be ready to dispute unfair chargebacks when they happen, which is a pain but is doable.
- Prevent as many chargebacks as possible from happening in the first place.

About This Book

Chargebacks For Dummies, Chargebacks911 Special Edition, is your guide for preventing chargebacks and, when they happen, fighting them more effectively. It provides a full understanding of what chargebacks are, who makes them happen, why they happen, and what you can do about them.

This book was prepared by experts in the field of chargeback prevention and disputation. It's based on years of experience in the business of getting a handle on the chargeback problem.

Flip through the pages to find tips for improving your business practices and fighting the good fight. You'll find out why you need some expert help to win this war.

Foolish Assumptions

In preparing this book, I've made some assumptions about you, the reader:

» You're a merchant of some kind, providing great goods or excellent services, quite possibly marketing them online.

» You know your business well, and want to focus on growing your business rather than battling the ugly red tape known as chargebacks.

» You'd like some background on the topic to help you learn what you can do, and when to call for help.

Icons Used in This Book

This book is intended to be easy to read and easy to navigate. That's why these cute little icons appear in the margins:

REMEMBER

If you don't have time to pore over every word, at least pay special attention to the paragraphs marked with this icon.

TIP

You need both knowledge and advice about chargebacks. This icon identifies a helpful tip.

WARNING

If you're selling retail goods or services, you already know what a threat chargebacks can be. Here's one more warning to keep in mind.

> **IN THIS CHAPTER**
>
> » **Understanding the chargeback concept**
>
> » **Learning how chargebacks came about**
>
> » **Meeting the major players in the process**

Chapter 1
What's a Chargeback?

A lot of things compel people to go into business. The spark is typically a great idea, a "light bulb" moment for a product or service that is better or more innovative than what's out there now. It's a passion for success, a thrill at being on the cutting edge. It's a desire to make a living, or even to get rich.

It's a good bet that no one goes into business for the joy of dealing with red tape and paperwork. Collecting money is a necessary evil and a reward for hard work, but few people enjoy the process. This chapter outlines one part of the process that's especially unattractive: the chargeback that takes money from your account rather than putting it in. This chapter discusses the reasons chargebacks were invented and introduces the major players in the chargeback saga.

Defining Chargebacks

REMEMBER

At its core, a chargeback is essentially the reverse of a charge. When a customer buys a product or service from you using a charge card, money flows from the customer into your account as the merchant. In a *chargeback,* money that had been deposited into your account is taken back out, and the customer gets a credit.

That may sound a lot like a refund, but it isn't. Here are some key differences that show how a chargeback is anything but a refund:

- **A chargeback is often a surprise.** With a refund, the customer has returned the product or notified you of a concern, and you have agreed to refund some or all of the purchase price. You're in the driver's seat. With a chargeback, by contrast, you often have no idea that the customer or the bank has an issue with the transaction.

- **You're totally in the dark.** Because you're the one initiating a refund, you know when the funds will be removed from your account and returned to the customer. In the case of a chargeback, you're likely to be caught off guard when that forced withdrawal happens and the money vanishes from your account.

- **You lose your second chance for a sale.** With a refund for a product, you usually get the product back, and as long as there was nothing wrong with it, you can sell it to someone else. With a chargeback, you typically don't get the product back, which means you're out the cost of the product and any potential for profit.

- **You're hit with extra fees.** When you refund money to a customer, you still owe the fees associated with the original transaction. That's a drag, but a chargeback is worse, because you lose those original fees and on top of that, you have to pay a chargeback fee. Double whammy!

- **Your reputation is tarnished.** Refunds happen. It's just part of doing business, and those who process your charges know that. They take a dim view of chargebacks, however. Each time a chargeback happens, it's a black mark on your reputation. If it happens too many times, your permission to process credit card transactions can be revoked, which might wipe out your ability to operate.

Understanding How Chargebacks Came into Existence

As you read this book, you may come away thinking chargeback is a four-letter word (even if it actually has ten letters). Indeed, chargebacks can be a menace to the health of your business.

But they were originally created to serve a worthwhile purpose, and the concept still has its merits.

REMEMBER

Chargebacks were created as a means for consumer protection. In the United States, they were included in the 1974 Fair Credit Billing Act, and they became part of the legal structure in other countries, too, as card network regulations took shape.

Consumer protection, on the surface, is certainly not a bad thing. Chargebacks were intended to protect consumers in two ways, and these two benefits remain important today:

- » **Protection against criminals:** If someone steals your credit card (or the numbers on it), you aren't held responsible for unauthorized transactions. That helps you feel better about having a card in the first place, knowing that it's safe from criminal fraud. You can even argue that this safety net helped make online commerce happen, because no one would want to buy online if there weren't protections against the bad guys.

- » **Protection against unsavory business practices:** Because forced refunds can happen, merchants have an incentive to be honest and provide quality goods or services. You, as a merchant, also have good reason to pay attention to customer complaints and resolve them effectively and efficiently, lest the customer take the matter to the bank. This protection also has historically worked to encourage credit card commerce, so you might argue that it helps you as a merchant.

That's the bright side. For every silver lining, though, there's a cloud. Customers are getting more and more savvy about the use of chargebacks. Some think pursuing a chargeback through the bank will be easier than getting a refund from you, the merchant. To them, a chargeback is sort of a lazy person's refund.

WARNING

Some of the less honest folks out there believe that if they play their cards right with chargebacks, they can get free stuff. Some people call this growing practice *friendly fraud*, though it's anything but friendly to your business operations. There's more on this topic in Chapter 3.

How Chargebacks Happen Now

REMEMBER

A chargeback can be requested by the customer, or it may be initiated by the bank. If it's the customer's idea, it may happen soon after the transaction, or it can occur days or even months later. All that it takes is for the customer to contact the issuing bank — the one that issued the credit or debit card — and complain about the transaction. It may be a legitimate dispute, but in many cases, it isn't. Either way, the money disappears from your account.

Why would the bank initiate a chargeback? That happens when there's a discrepancy with the transaction. Discrepancies often occur with transactions that should not have gone through in the first place. Here are some possible causes:

» **The authorization was declined.** Sometimes a transaction is processed even after the issuing bank has declined to authorize it.

» **There was no authorization.** In this case, a transaction was processed even though an authorization was not even sought.

» **The card was expired.** The expiration date on the card had passed but the transaction was processed anyway (typically without an authorization).

» **It was a late presentment.** You, the merchant, did not process the transaction in a timely manner.

» **The account number is wrong.** The number presented didn't match any account that is on file.

Who's Involved in the Chargeback Process?

Before going any deeper into the saga of chargebacks, it's worth getting to know the major players in this increasingly dangerous drama. It takes a whole cast of characters to make chargebacks happen. Roll the credits!

- **The cardholder:** It takes a customer to write the beginning of the story. The *cardholder* sees something he or she wants to buy, pulls out a charge card, and either swipes it or types it into an ecommerce website. So far, so good. The drama begins when the cardholder disputes the transaction by requesting a chargeback.

- **The card network:** The whole business of credit card commerce would not happen without such big names as Visa, Mastercard, American Express, and Discover. These are all examples of *card networks,* also known as *card associations* or *schemes*. They set up the guidelines that make it all work.

- **The issuing bank:** Two banks are involved in processing a credit card transaction. The first is the *issuing bank* or *issuer*. This bank provides the payment card to the customer. The issuing bank is a member of the card network, and is the entity that deals directly with the customer (the customer may have a Visa card or a Mastercard piece of plastic, but does not interact directly with the card network).

- **The acquiring bank:** Sometimes called the *acquirer* or the *merchant bank,* the *acquiring bank* represents you, the merchant. This bank is also a member of the card network and does the direct dealing with the network so that you don't have to. The acquiring bank provides the merchant account that allows you to accept credit card payments.

- **The payment processor:** The story of a credit card transaction could never happen without all the players, but this character does the bulk of the work in making the transaction happen. The *payment processor,* which has a connection to the acquiring bank, collects the information needed to complete the transaction and moves the funds from the issuing bank to the acquiring bank. It verifies available funds and authorizes payments, and it's on the lookout for fraud. In the case of a chargeback, the payment processor moves the funds back from the acquiring bank to the issuing bank.

- **The payment gateway:** This player is software that connects the merchant with the banks, stepping in to help make the transaction happen. The payment gateway communicates essential information to the payment processor, facilitating the deal.

FAST FACTS ABOUT CREDIT CARD USAGE

It should come as no surprise to learn that there are a lot of credit cards out there, and a lot of credit card holders. According to the Federal Reserve, some 70 percent of American adults carry plastic, and consumer surveys have found that those cardholders each carry an average of 3.7 cards.

Cards — either credit or debit — are used in the majority of transactions across all kinds of businesses. A 2016 TSYS study found that only 9 percent of department store buyers pay in cash, but two-thirds use credit or debit cards. Even more grocery story shoppers use plastic.

Discount store customers pull out cash more often, but the percent that do are still in the minority. It's really only at the coffee shop and fast-food restaurants where cash users hold a plurality over those with credit cards and those with debit cards. Even so, fewer than half favor paper money and coins.

This probably isn't surprising either — when people pay with credit, they spend a lot more money than when they're using a debit card that draws upon funds they have in the bank. On average, consumers spend 237 percent more when they're using credit cards, compared with debit cards.

In the U.S., the average credit card user runs 187 transactions per year. Collectively, they tally nearly 34 million card purchases every year.

> **IN THIS CHAPTER**
>
> » Filing the claim
> » Moving the money
> » Disputing the chargeback
> » Learning the verdict
> » Understanding the timetable

Chapter 2
The Chargeback Process

The chargeback process is a bit like a legal case. But the "innocent until proven guilty" concept doesn't entirely apply. As a merchant, you're going to see your dollars disappear right away when a chargeback is filed, and from that point on you're battling to get your money back.

This chapter outlines the chargeback process, from the initial complaint to the transfer of funds, to the dispute, to the verdict.

The Initial Claim

As explained in Chapter 1, the difference between a chargeback and a refund starts near the beginning of the process. Either way, the customer gets things going by issuing a complaint. In the case of a refund, the customer complains to you, the merchant. You're the one who then initiates the movement of funds from your account back to the customer. With a chargeback, the customer complains to the bank, and you as the merchant might not even know there's a problem.

REMEMBER

How that initial chargeback communication takes place depends on policies established by the issuer, but it often is pretty simple. It can even be a telephone call, in which an agent for the bank walks the cardholder through the process right then and there.

In other cases, the cardholder is instructed to file a written complaint. This can be pretty simple, depending on the issuer. It may be a letter in the mail, or it may be as simple as sending an email or filling out an online form. Some issuers require some sort of supporting documentation, such as a sales receipt or a copy of email communications between the cardholder and the merchant, but many don't.

The point is that, even at its most complex, the process of disputing a transaction with the bank isn't terribly difficult. It's so hassle-free, in fact, that many customers believe it's easier than getting a refund the old-fashioned way, by contacting the merchant. Those cardholders who have done this enough times have figured out the loopholes.

WARNING

Here's one of those loopholes that some people figure out if they're experienced: Banks often take the cardholder's word and don't bother to do much research into the claim. Some do the homework, of course, and if the issuing bank finds the claim doesn't have much substance, the bank rejects it right off the bat. But more often than not, the claim proceeds.

As a general rule, the bank expects the customer to first try to resolve the matter with the merchant. In fact, that's the protocol established by card networks, and both banks and customers presumably agree to follow the rule.

But research suggests that this contact with the merchant happens in only one of seven cases. Most issuers follow the old adage that "The customer is always right." Why? Consider that the average customer makes a card purchase at least every other day. That's a pretty consistent relationship between cardholder and bank, and banks don't want to jeopardize that relationship.

The problem is, that's the kind of attitude that encourages unscrupulous customers who want to get free stuff from merchants like you. And just to say it like it is, "free stuff" is a euphemism — customers who do this kind of thing on purpose are stealing.

Certainly, most customers aren't crooks, but those who figure out how easy it is to file a fraudulent claim stand a good chance of making a habit of it. As many as half of cardholders who file a fraudulent chargeback do so again within two months. Banks that look the other way are enabling this lawlessness.

As mentioned in Chapter 1, an issuing bank can initiate a chargeback for quite a few different reasons. There are multiple explanations for a customer-requested chargeback, and there are quite a few more reasons the bank itself might get the ball rolling. How do you find out the reason why this bummer is happening? The chargeback is assigned a reason code.

REMEMBER

The *reason code* is exactly what it sounds like. The card networks compile a list of all possible reasons for a chargeback, and each reason gets its own code. Knowing the reason helps you determine what to do about the chargeback, and potentially, how to prevent similar chargebacks from happening in the future.

The Transfer of Funds

Here's where things get difficult for you, the merchant. Once the issuing bank decides the cardholder's claim is valid, it applies a temporary credit to the cardholder's account. That money doesn't grow on a tree somewhere — it comes straight from your bank account as the merchant. What if the bank didn't research the details of the claim? That doesn't matter — the money is coming out of your account, pronto.

WARNING

That forced withdrawal may, in fact, be the first clue you get that this customer is seeking his or her money back. Merchants are often caught off guard by chargebacks. No one needs to tell you how much trouble it can cause for your cash flow when money you had in your account suddenly vanishes.

But wait — there's more! Not only does the purchase amount disappear from your balance; so does the amount of the chargeback fee. When you sign up for a merchant account with the acquiring bank, you get a list of the terms of service, and those terms include a chargeback fee. How much that fee is depends on the bank, but it typically ranges anywhere from $20 to $100 for each chargeback.

The Dispute

If that transfer of funds were the end of the story, that would clearly be grossly unfair to you, the merchant. Just as the cardholder has the right to file for a chargeback, you have a right to fight back and dispute the claim. That doesn't mean it's easy.

REMEMBER

The process of disputing a chargeback is known as *representment*. Note that Visa has recently begun calling this stage *dispute response/pre-arbitration*. Why a dispute response? Because Visa also is shifting terminology such that a *chargeback* is to become known as a *dispute* (and thus, your representment is a response to that dispute).

Whether your card network uses the term *representment* or not, the term is helpful in understanding what's going on here. You are essentially re-presenting the transaction to the issuing bank, asking the bank to honor the original transaction. You are re-presenting the transaction, along with some sort of evidence that supports your side of the story. Your evidence should support your view that the charge was fair and reasonable, and should be allowed to go through.

As in any court case, you need compelling evidence to successfully dispute a chargeback. What kind of evidence you present depends on the reason code assigned to the chargeback, as well as the rules set forth in your agreement with the card network. In general, you're hoping to show proof that the customer agreed to the terms of the sale, knew what he or she was doing in making the purchase, and authorized the transaction.

Here are some examples of evidence that may be requested in the representment or dispute response process:

>> Order forms indicating that the customer ordered the product

>> Delivery confirmation proving that it was delivered and signed for by the customer

>> Photos or emails proving that the cardholder received the service or has the item

>> Communications from the customer showing that he or she was satisfied with the purchase

TIP Along with the evidence, you need to attach a persuasive letter explaining the evidence and outlining your defense. The more professional the letter, the better.

The Final Decision

Once you've filed your representment or dispute response, the ball is in the issuing bank's court. What happens next? You win some and you lose some. Here are the possibilities:

» **You win.** Congratulations! You persuaded the issuing bank by presenting sufficiently compelling evidence. The temporary credit is removed from the cardholder's account, and the funds go back into your account. This is known as a *chargeback reversal,* or using Visa's new terminology, a *dispute reversal.* Either way, you're unfortunately still out the chargeback fee.

» **You lose.** Your representment evidence did not convince the issuer to cancel the chargeback. The temporary credit in the cardholder's account becomes permanent, and that is that. Better luck next time!

» **Not so fast. . . .** Rather than overturn or confirm the chargeback, the issuer may file a second chargeback. It means the case isn't closed. Sometimes a second chargeback happens because the issuer has changed the chargeback code or gotten new information from the customer. It might mean that the evidence didn't match the reason code. The bottom line is that the customer still wants to dispute the transaction, or the bank has decided to follow a different course.

If the case heads down the arbitration path, it often means you need even more evidence. As with the original decision, the arbitration process allows review of the evidence and an ultimate determination in favor of either the cardholder or the merchant. The card network is responsible for making the final, final decision.

Time Is of the Essence

REMEMBER

Sometimes the chargeback process is simple. The customer may have simply forgotten making the purchase, and once you can show a sales receipt, that's all it takes to resolve the dispute. In those cases, the acquiring bank may already have what's needed to take care of the situation. Unfortunately, most chargeback disputes are more complicated and time-consuming.

REMEMBER

Therein is the problem. Disputing chargebacks takes time, and if you're like most merchants, that's something you have precious little of. Not only does it take a fair amount of time, it has to be done right away. Usually, you have only a few days to file a representment or dispute response once you've been notified of a chargeback. That doesn't leave you much time to gather the evidence and prepare your submission.

On top of that, the process and the terminology are anything but straightforward. Odds are you'll come across terms you've never seen before or that don't make sense to you. There isn't even a single set of jargon for you to learn, because one card network's terminology is often different from another's. Certainly, the lists of reason codes are different depending on the card network.

Is it really worth all the trouble? Some merchants throw their hands into the air and give up, and just assume chargebacks are part of the cost of doing business. They know that every minute they spend dealing with chargebacks is a minute they've been distracted from the important work of running and growing the operation.

REMEMBER

The answer is, yes, it's worth dealing with chargebacks. You just need a good system and the right help.

> **IN THIS CHAPTER**
> » Fighting criminal fraud
> » Resolving merchant errors
> » Getting something for nothing

Chapter 3
Why Chargebacks Happen

Chargebacks happen for many reasons, and not all of them are indefensible. They're a remedy for criminal fraud, which is good for the consumer (albeit a bummer for the merchant). And they are one way to fix merchant error (although there are certainly better ways). Most chargebacks these days, though, are for reasons that are a whole lot less valid.

This chapter spells out the reasons chargebacks happen, from criminal fraud to merchant error to the problem euphemistically known as friendly fraud. Hint: You're not going to think friendly fraud is the least bit friendly.

Reason 1: Criminal Fraud

As mentioned in Chapter 1, the system of chargebacks dates back to the 1974 Fair Credit Billing Act. Chargebacks were created as a protection for consumers, and it's a protection that helps cardholders feel more comfortable doing business using their plastic.

REMEMBER

Unless you've been residing under a rock, you've heard lots about the ever-growing threat of cybercrime. As many as half of Americans have been the victim of some variety of card fraud in the past few years. Chargebacks help cardholders get their money back when their card is used fraudulently.

How can cybercrime be so prevalent, when there are so many sophisticated ways of preventing it? Unfortunately, cybercriminals are just as sophisticated as the good guys, and they adapt well to the safeguards put in place to stop them.

WARNING

For example, digital fingerprinting is not as effective as it used to be in shining the light on suspicious activities. Those intent on committing fraud can thwart identifiers such as cookies when they're making an unauthorized purchase.

The bad guys are also getting better at altering computer characteristics, which makes IP location intelligence all but worthless. It used to be that location information could help mitigate fraud, but this information can easily be compromised through location masking.

The other problem is that merchants are hesitant to adopt prevention tactics that get in the way of legitimate business. If your antifraud tactics make the user experience too difficult, you end up driving shoppers away. But a less robust approach leaves holes for fraudsters to drive through.

Here are some of the ways criminals are getting their hands on credit card information:

» **Phishing:** This is an effort to get users to give away their personal financial information through fraudulent emails or social media. Users click a link that leads to a faked web page in which they unwittingly enter their card numbers or passwords. It's easy for criminals to cast a wide phishing net, but some of the more sophisticated attacks are known as *spear phishing*. In these cases, the crook digs up enough detail to personalize the attack and go after a specific individual.

» **Malware:** Phishing attacks can spread malware that quietly collects sensitive data and passes it along to the bad guys. Malware can also wind up on computers and mobile devices through malicious app downloads.

- **Skimmers:** These devices copy the information from a credit card's magnetic strip. Fraudsters install them on gas pumps, automated teller machines, and other point-of-sale terminals, and collect vital information while users are making legitimate transactions.

- **Radio frequency identification (RFID) hacks:** Many cards store RFID information so that users can tap them rather than swipe them at the point of payment. This innovation is handy for customers, but that RFID information can be hacked if a criminal places a special device near the user.

REMEMBER

Now for the big surprise. Fraud was one of the reasons chargebacks were created in the first place, and who could argue against using chargebacks to remedy fraud cases? As big a problem as cybercrime is, you'd think it would be the biggest reason chargebacks happen, but in reality, only 10 percent of chargebacks are the result of criminal fraud.

Even More Common: Merchant Error

REMEMBER

Nobody's perfect. Most people can agree on that. Merchants do, from time to time, make mistakes. In fact, about one in five chargebacks is the result of an error made by the merchant.

A potential merchant error is neglecting to cancel a recurring transaction when the customer has asked to be canceled. Or perhaps there was an error in entering the transaction amount, or the shipping address. It's certainly possible the customer was overcharged because someone goofed, or that the shipment was sent to the wrong place. It's usually an innocent mistake, not an intentional scam, of course. But little mistakes can blossom into big problems.

TIP

If merchants can make mistakes, that means it's possible to make fewer mistakes. Perhaps you can prevent some of your chargebacks by improving your processes — it's likely worth the trouble. Adopting best practices and ensuring that they're followed reduces your chargeback rate.

You can argue that filing a chargeback is not the best way to resolve a merchant error. From the merchant's perspective, it would be much better if the customer made contact with the merchant, rather than dragging the banks into the dispute.

Alas, some people are uncomfortable with such a straightforward approach, and instead go straight for the chargeback. In other cases, the customer tries to get the merchant to fix the problem, but isn't satisfied with the resolution.

And then, there are the times when a customer asks for a chargeback and blames the merchant, although the merchant isn't at fault. The chargeback reason codes used most often to indicate merchant error also happen to be commonly used for friendly fraud.

The Biggest Reason: Friendly Fraud

REMEMBER

So, criminal fraud causes 10 percent of chargebacks, and merchant error results in 20 percent. There's 70 percent left, and that 70 percent is the result of what's known as *friendly fraud* or *chargeback fraud*. It's a huge problem.

It's a big bucket, and a few different kinds of situations fall into it. Some are more innocent-seeming than others, but all amount to getting a refund outside of the normal, honest refund process. Even if the customer simply felt like taking the "easy way out" by calling the bank rather than the merchant, the customer is guilty of friendly fraud.

If it sounds harsh to suggest that these kinds of lazy customers are committing fraud, don't forget that they're essentially getting something for free when they get their money back through a chargeback rather than a traditional refund. It may not be something they ended up wanting, or it was the wrong size or color. But the fact remains that when they go the chargeback route, the item in question remains in their possession rather than being returned to the merchant to be sold to someone else.

That's what makes these chargebacks fraud. Chargebacks may have been born as a consumer protection, but they've turned into a no-hassle way to get money back. Not only is it sometimes easier to transact the matter through the bank agent rather than the merchant, for an online purchase it saves the hassle of shipping the product back to the merchant. Convenient, maybe, but it's no better than shoplifting.

Here are the four main situations that collectively make up the problem of friendly fraud:

- **Buyer's remorse:** The customer changes his or her mind about the purchase. Maybe the purchase was a bit of a whim, such as a pricey piece of home decor, and the buyer decides later that it would be more prudent not to spend that much money on something so whimsical. It's a normal occurrence, but in this case the customer decides it's easier to call the bank than to deal with the merchant.

- **Reining in a spouse:** A primary cardholder doesn't like a purchase another family member made. In this case, it's the spouse who found that pricey piece of home decor to be a bit too whimsical and imprudent from a financial perspective. So the spouse calls the bank rather than getting the buyer to take the item back.

- **Bending the refund rules:** Most retailers have a time limit for getting a return, often 30 days. Some buyers miss the deadline — perhaps they bought the item early as a gift and it wasn't even unwrapped until after the deadline. So the buyer or recipient tries to get around the deadline policy by filing a chargeback.

- **Something for nothing:** In the worst cases, the buyer wants the item but never intended to pay for it. That pricey piece of home decor? Maybe the plan all along was to acquire it, then request a chargeback. The buyer in this case plans to keep the item but take it easy on the budget by not paying for it. A chargeback becomes an avenue for free stuff.

REMEMBER

If you check the lists of reason codes in the appendix at the back of this book, you'll have a hard time finding any of these reasons listed. That's because they aren't valid reasons for chargebacks. Customers getting chargebacks for these reasons need to make up an excuse for wanting their money back, often a reason suggesting merchant error. Now you can see why this practice is considered fraud.

Friendly fraud is incredibly costly for you, the merchant. Just as in cases of shoplifting, you end up losing an item from your inventory with no money in the bank to show for it. Service businesses, meanwhile, don't have to deal with shoplifting (it isn't possible to shoplift car repair or housecleaning), but chargebacks can make them feel like they've been robbed. On top of the lost product or service effort, they have to pay a chargeback fee. To learn more about the costs to businesses, turn to Chapter 4.

Fraudsters Are Taking a Risk

What cardholders may not realize is that they can become a victim of their own friendly fraud, too. Engaging in chargeback fraud is not without risk. Here are some of the risks that they have unwittingly volunteered to take:

» **The fees:** If the bank declines the chargeback request or the cardholder loses out to the compelling evidence supplied by the merchant, the cardholder may be required to pay the processing fees. Oops!

» **The cutoff:** Cardholders determined to have filed fraudulent chargebacks may end up having their credit card account terminated by the bank. That's more than just an inconvenience. It can cause a downgrade of their credit score.

» **The price we all pay:** Retailers do everything they can to stop shoplifting, but in the end it becomes one of the costs of doing business. That cost gets added into the price of every product, which means honest people are hurt by shoplifting. As chargeback fraud continues to become more and more of a problem, you can expect the cost of chargeback fraud to become a bigger component of the sticker price. That hurts all of us (even chargeback fraudsters, who have to buy and actually pay for things now and then).

> **IN THIS CHAPTER**
> » Calculating the cost of chargebacks
> » Understanding the threat
> » Taking a reputation hit

Chapter 4
How Chargebacks Hurt Merchants

You've designed and built a better mousetrap, or you've created a unique retail experience with an irresistible lineup of products. Those are the keys to success, for sure, but you can still crash by the end of the journey if you don't get a handle on chargebacks.

This chapter outlines why you need to care about chargebacks just as much as you care about your product, service, or inventory. It spells out the costs of chargebacks — not only the cost in dollars, but the hits you can take in your reputation and even in your ability to survive in the long term.

Chargebacks Cost a Lot

WARNING

Chargebacks hit you in the bottom line in a number of ways. They are a significant cost issue, and if you haven't experienced the brunt of this problem yet, there's every chance you might down the road:

» **Loss of the product:** This one hurts. It's certainly a drag when someone returns a product that you thought you had successfully sold, and you have to go to the trouble of putting the item back into your inventory. But all is not lost. At least you have the product and can try to sell it to someone else. However, if you sell someone a product and that buyer successfully files a chargeback, the item is gone forever, and so is the money that the customer paid for it. You lose, big time!

» **Double the fees:** Merchants often complain about the interchange and assessment fees associated with card transactions, but most accept them grudgingly as a cost of doing business in today's environment. The problem is, you don't get those fees back when there's a chargeback. Instead, you get another fee: the chargeback fee. You also don't get back what it cost you to ship the product to the customer.

» **The markup:** A chargeback fee is a bad enough problem, but the truth is, this fee gets passed around. It can be passed from one entity to another, getting repriced along the way, and by the time it hits your bottom line, it may be multiple times what it was when the chargeback started. Ouch!

» **Your valuable time:** Whether you win or lose in a chargeback case, if you decide to fight it, it's costing you the time you spend dealing with it.

Chargebacks Threaten Your Lifeblood

Chargebacks are a pain for everyone involved, except perhaps the friendly fraudster. In fact, they're a pain for banks and card networks, too. Chargebacks carry a cost in terms of administrative burden, and they can eat into profits. You aren't the only one who wants to reduce chargebacks; so do the other players in this drama.

WARNING

That's why card networks have chargeback management programs. They keep track of which merchants have the biggest chargeback problems, and you don't want to be one of those businesses on the "naughty" list. You can be hit with significant fines, and in severe cases, you may even lose your ability to process cards. Depending on what your business is, that can be a real killer.

Card networks keep track of your chargebacks by calculating a chargeback ratio. It's pretty simple math, really. Your ratio is the number of first chargebacks filed this month divided by total transactions. Mastercard uses total transactions last month as the denominator; Visa uses total transactions in the current month.

WARNING

That mention of a "naughty" list is not a joke. These lists exist. For example, Mastercard's *MATCH (Member Alert to Control High-Risk) list* is a list of businesses and business owners whose privileges to process card transactions have been terminated.

The MATCH list helps acquiring banks screen for high-risk merchants. Being on the list doesn't necessarily mean you will be forbidden from accepting plastic, but you may have to get your merchant account from a bank that specializes in high-risk merchants, and that costs you more.

Several factors can mess up your card acceptance privileges and land you on the MATCH list, including bankruptcy, money laundering, and fraud convictions. Those are certainly no-no's that are within your control. But another thing on the list is excessive chargebacks. So, be aware of the risk!

Chargebacks Can Look Bad

Your level of chargeback activity can negatively affect your reputation in the eyes of acquiring banks. You need a merchant account from an acquiring bank, and it's going to be classified as either a low-risk account or a high-risk account.

The ideal situation is to get a low-risk account with a traditional bank. However, if your operation is deemed too risky, you're forced to work with a processor that specializes in high-risk accounts. These processors charge significantly higher rates, and that's bad for the health of your business.

REMEMBER

How is your risk determined, especially if you don't have a track record of chargeback activity? The bank evaluates your risk based on a number of factors known to influence the risk of chargebacks. Here are some examples:

>> Businesses selling some kinds of products or providing certain kinds of services are more at risk than others.

CHAPTER 4 **How Chargebacks Hurt Merchants** 23

- » The methods you use to sell make a difference. Standard marketing tactics such as search engine optimization are seen as less risky than, say, affiliate marketing.
- » How you process transactions is important, too. If you mainly handle card-present transactions, those tend to have a lower risk of chargebacks than card-not-present transactions.
- » Your average monthly sales and the average of your individual transactions have an impact on your chargeback risk.
- » Sales into certain countries are more likely to spark chargebacks.

Your costs are certainly lower if you're deemed to be a low-risk merchant, you're selling low-risk products, and your customers live in lower-risk countries. That philosophy suits most companies just fine.

REMEMBER

That said, some businesses are not troubled by being declared higher-risk. Remember the conventional wisdom about risks and rewards. You may have a potential for higher rewards if you're willing to operate in higher-risk settings (and if the costs don't throw your bottom line for a loop).

One high-risk situation you may decide is worth it is entering a new foreign market. Generally, the United States, Canada, Japan, Australia, Western Europe, and Northern Europe are not seen as risky markets. You may decide there's enough money to be made somewhere else that it's worth the cost of high-risk fees.

If you're in the business of recurring payments, that may also be considered high-risk. But lining up a bunch of regular monthly charge payments is a pretty sweet deal, often seen as lucrative enough to make higher fees worth it.

No matter which world you operate in — low-risk or high-risk — it pays to minimize chargebacks as much as possible. If you have reasons to operate in a riskier setting, that's up to you, but you shouldn't have to earn that distinction solely on the basis of chargebacks.

> **IN THIS CHAPTER**
> » Sorting through the confusion
> » Playing on a field that isn't level
> » Facing more opportunities for fraud
> » Fearing the holidays

Chapter 5
Why the Chargeback Battle Is So Difficult

This chapter spells out some of the reasons chargebacks often get the best of merchants. Chargebacks are confusing, the rules are less than fair to merchants, and the bad guys keep getting better at their dirty work. To make matters worse, the most lucrative time of year for retailers happens to be a big time for chargebacks.

Chargebacks Are Confusing

From a merchant's perspective, chargebacks can be confusing for three main reasons:

» **You may not have fully acknowledged the problem.** Acknowledging a problem is, after all, the first step to solving it.

» **You don't have all the information you need to correctly identify the problem.**

» **As a result, you're taking the wrong approach to tackling chargebacks.** The good news is, you picked up this book, so you're on the road toward a more helpful approach.

Consumers can be confused by chargebacks, too. It would be wrong to assume that all cardholders set out to be crooks when they file a potentially fraudulent chargeback. The fact is, many simply have no idea what they're doing.

REMEMBER

For example, one Chargebacks911 survey found that 49 percent of consumers didn't know they were filing a chargeback. They thought they could call up their bank for help dealing with the merchant. Some thought they could call the bank and ask to have a recurring subscription canceled. They didn't specifically request a chargeback, but that's the tool available to the bank.

The same survey found that most consumers had filed a chargeback purely for convenience. They thought it would be less time-consuming to deal with the bank. Most of these respondents likely don't think of themselves as thieves, but the fact is, they're taking something for nothing.

The Playing Field Is Not Level

Read this book or live through the experience of being a merchant for a while. Either way, you're likely to exclaim, "Chargebacks are just not fair!" You're right. Merchants frequently get the bad end of the deal.

REMEMBER

The main players in the chargeback story have unequal levels of power. The merchant has pretty much everything to lose. The cardholder has virtually everything to gain. Then you have the card network and the issuing bank, who are happiest when these little inconveniences just go away with as little trouble as possible.

WARNING

Because card networks and issuing banks benefit from fast resolution, they're likely to make things happen quickly. They get what they want. A speedy resolution tends to benefit the cardholder at the expense of the merchant.

The bottom line is many consumers are filing illegitimate chargebacks, and banks don't have adequate resources to weed out all the bad claims.

HORRIFYING CHARGEBACK FACTS

Familiarity with chargebacks breeds more chargebacks. Once a customer successfully files a chargeback, he or she views it as a new tool in the shopping toolkit. A customer who has succeeded in a chargeback case is nine times more likely to file another one.

These repeat chargebacks happen quickly, too. Of those customers who file a chargeback for questionable reasons and see that it isn't challenged, half try again within a couple of months.

Some chargebacks are reasonable because they're a response to criminal fraud or merchant error. But these understandable chargebacks are in the minority. Most chargebacks are much less valid. That said, fewer than 20 percent of ecommerce merchants regularly dispute invalid chargebacks, also known as *friendly fraud*. For those in ecommerce, friendly fraud makes up 85 percent of their chargebacks.

Chargebacks are becoming harder and harder to ignore, though. The financial impact of chargebacks may approach $30 billion by 2020. Meanwhile, fraud in general continues to rise. The share of total revenue lost to fraud was up 279 percent from 2013 to 2016.

Chances for Fraud Are Growing

Who uses cash anymore? Coins and paper money are fast becoming quaint. The last holdouts for cash seemed to be fast-food restaurants, vending machines, and parking meters, but more and more of these transactions are card-enabled, too.

That's good news for consumers, but it means the opportunities for fraud are vastly increasing, too — both criminal fraud and friendly fraud. That opens the door for more and more chargebacks.

WARNING

Card-not-present transactions are especially vulnerable to fraud, and they're growing fast. They're growing much faster than the technology for fraud detection and prevention. The more fraud, the more the need for chargebacks.

Unhappy Holidays

Retailers live for the holidays. Many earn a large share of their year's sales and profits in November and December as people splurge on gifts for others, or spend gift dollars they have received. On Black Friday weekend, shoppers spend hundreds of dollars on average.

That all sounds like good news, and there's no reason it shouldn't be. But more transactions mean more opportunity for chargebacks. More people are buying things that will be returned, and not all of those returns will go through the proper refund channels. More impulsive purchases can lead to more buyer's remorse.

WARNING

A great November and December can lead to a big chargeback hangover in January and February. It's an unsettling confluence of increased friendly fraud and an uptick in criminal fraud that's enabled by the hectic pace of holiday retailing. That pace also can cause an increase in merchant errors, which means even more chargebacks.

It's a perfectly terrible storm for merchants. Because there are so many chargebacks, you're more likely to let some of them slide. And in some cases, holiday chargebacks can be even more expensive than usual. Consider that when you lose a sale through a chargeback, you lose the product, you're out the fees, and you don't get back the shipping cost, either. But during the holidays, there's often an increase in the use of express shipping, which means the shipping costs you lose may be pricier than normal.

TIP

Don't take it as a "bah humbug" for the holiday retailing season, though. It's more like a wakeup call to ensure that you hone your chargeback strategy before the holidays hit. You need to prevent as many chargebacks as you can, and be ready to deal effectively with the ones you can't prevent.

IN THIS CHAPTER

» Preventing chargebacks

» Disputing chargebacks effectively

» Deciding to hire an expert

Chapter 6
The Merchants Strike Back

This chapter lays the groundwork for doing something about chargebacks. It summarizes ways you can prevent them from happening in the first place, spells out why it's worth disputing them when they happen, offers tips for disputing successfully, and discusses the reasons for getting expert help.

Preventing Chargebacks

Chargebacks are a pain in the you-know-what, so a great place to exert some effort is keeping them from happening in the first place. There are two big reasons why preventing chargebacks is so important.

REMEMBER

You need chargeback prevention because every chargeback you fail to prevent is going to cost you a lot of money. Not only that, you can lose your merchant account if you experience too many chargebacks, and that can choke off the lifeblood of your business.

Verifying the buyer

TIP

Lots of tools are available to help you detect and prevent fraud. The Address Verification Service (AVS) is an excellent one, because it helps you ensure that the person making a purchase is really the person who owns the card. Before you process a transaction, check with AVS to ensure that the billing address matches what the bank has on file.

Also quite helpful are card security codes, those three- or four-digit numbers on the back (or sometimes the front) of the credit card. This is information that's only available on the card, so if your buyer is able to provide it accurately, that means it's much more likely that the buyer has the card in hand and isn't using a stolen card number.

A 3D Secure code is similar, and all of the big card networks offer some variation of this concept. It's a predetermined code that the buyer must enter. Like the card security code, this isn't going to be available on a list of hacked numbers.

Satisfying the customer

Another key to preventing chargebacks is keeping the customer happy. The happier customers are, the less likely they'll want a refund or a chargeback.

TIP

Happy customers know what they want and receive exactly what they expect. That requires you to provide accurate descriptions of what you're selling. Choose your words with care, with no jargon or hyperbole. Provide plenty of images so the customer can inspect the product.

Making billing clear

TIP

A confusing bill can also cause an unhappy customer, so pay attention to your *billing descriptor* — the way your company's identifying information appears on the customer's billing statement. If your customer sees a listing on the card statement and can't easily figure out what it was, the transaction may turn into a chargeback.

Your customer-service policies can make or break customer satisfaction. Be certain your customers know about the shipping process so they won't be surprised or disappointed.

Also, be sure your refund policy is clear, reasonable, and easy to find, or else your customer may ask for a chargeback instead of a refund.

Staying connected

Certainly, keeping customers happy won't stop those who try to use chargebacks in order to get free stuff. But better communication can help. Plenty of customers wind up in the middle of a chargeback because they had a problem and thought calling the bank was the best way to proceed.

TIP

Give the customer plenty of options besides flipping their card over and calling the number on the back. Make sure *your* contact information is even easier for them to find — on your website, on all correspondence, everywhere.

One other way to connect is to use a chargeback alert system. If a customer files a chargeback, you get an alert suggesting that you immediately reach out to the customer. Act fast, and you can stop a chargeback before it's finalized. In nearly every case, you'll have to give a refund, which is a bummer but is still better than a chargeback. You'll avoid chargeback fees and have the potential to get the product back.

Being responsive

Once you give the customer the ability to contact you, you need to be responsive and prompt. It helps to be human, too — customers appreciate speaking with a live person within four rings. Interactive voice response systems may improve your labor costs, but they can stand in the way of successful customer service.

If a customer emails you, make sure your system automatically acknowledges the email and says when the customer can expect to hear back. Then, meet that deadline. Also, keep an eye on your social media regularly, in case a customer reaches out that way.

People expect action much faster than they used to. One study found that virtually all customers expect to get a reply to their inquiry within 48 hours, but most want you to act even faster. More than a third want a response as fast as they can get a pizza delivered. You may need staff around the clock.

If a customer has an issue, be ready to offer a refund rather than an argument. If customers want to cancel service, let them. Otherwise they'll turn to the bank and you'll lose whatever power and goodwill you had.

Creating better processes

Given that recurring payments are a major source of chargeback pain, you should be able to prevent some chargebacks with better processes in this area. Be sure customers know they're buying into a recurring payment situation, and build better processes so that if they ask to opt out, you respond promptly.

It helps to send a reminder before you hit the customer's card with another recurring payment. That gives the customer time to cancel in advance if he or she no longer wants the service. If the rate for a recurring service is going up, let the customer know in advance.

Be sure your systems keep customers up to date on the fulfillment and shipping process, and make order-tracking easy for the customer. Also, be informative about backorders.

Disputing Chargebacks

No matter how hard you try to prevent them, chargebacks are going to slip through. Fewer of them, you hope, but it's unrealistic to imagine wiping them out completely. So, what to do? Dispute them!

You might say, "Of course I want to dispute chargebacks that aren't reasonable." Anyone with a sense of justice would want to fight an unjust chargeback, right?

You would think so, but not everyone does. Disputing a chargeback is time-consuming and costly, and it takes you away from the important business of running your business. Many reasonable people decide chargebacks are just an unfortunate part of doing business, and they decide to throw in the towel and live with the problem.

Here's an important, alternative view. If you build a history of fighting chargebacks, you may start seeing fewer chargebacks. Banks tend to issue fewer chargebacks against those merchants with a reputation of disputing them. They know you're not a pushover, so they think twice.

It's ironic. Banks, it turns out, don't like chargeback disputes any more than you do. Not fighting a chargeback saves you from the current dispute but it invites more chargebacks. On the other hand, fighting chargebacks today may reduce the number of disputes you face tomorrow.

REMEMBER

Here's another reason to dispute chargebacks when they're unjust — you're changing the big picture and the bottom line. You reduce your fees and cut your costs, and you may then have the option of cutting your prices. That, in turn, may win you more customers, and if your prices are lower, you might end up inspiring less buyer's remorse.

Finally, there is the business case. Chargebacks cost you money that you should not have lost in the first place. Get that money back, and your business may be a lot more profitable. Who doesn't want that?

Disputing Effectively

If you're going to effectively dispute a chargeback, you need a complete arsenal of weapons. The most effective weapons are documents that prove your case. If you wait to gather your weapons until the battle is on, though, you're going to find yourself at a disadvantage. You need to collect documentation all along so that it's at your fingertips when you need it.

TIP

That means organizing your chargeback effort from the very start. Your chargeback management system must be detailed, storing all pertinent information such as sales receipts, delivery confirmations, and email communications. It takes a lot of effort, and is well worth it.

You need speed, too. You don't have much time to dispute a chargeback, typically just a few days for creating a representment case, and you have to meet the deadlines.

You need a compelling letter. Documentation is essential, but it doesn't make a case on its own. That's where your letter comes in.

Finally, you need to be ready to learn. Disputing chargebacks is like any other skill — you'll get better at it the more you do it. You'll make mistakes, of course, and you'll learn from them. An unsuccessful chargeback representment offers clues that will help you succeed in the future.

Seeking Expert Help

Above all, you need an intensive chargeback management effort, and that isn't something that you can hatch overnight. You need some help.

REMEMBER

A chargeback expert helps you expose and prevent merchant errors that can turn into chargebacks. Your expert helps you outline necessary changes and implement best practices for preventing chargebacks and disputing them when they happen.

Your chargeback expert helps you lower your chargeback-to-transaction ratio and then keep it low. Because you hired an expert to handle most of this heavy lifting, you've saved your muscles for the tasks you do best: running your business and improving your revenue.

WARNING

Chargebacks can be a life-and-death issue for your business. That's because excessive chargeback levels threaten your merchant account and your ability to conduct card transactions. Lose that ability, and you might be out of business entirely.

Given that reality, you should consider excessive chargeback levels to be a true emergency. You need to drastically reduce your chargeback rate, and do so quickly. That is only feasible with professional help.

TIP

As you choose an expert, look for professionals who are on top of the industry's constant evolution. Chargeback threats change, and new threats emerge all the time. Fraudsters learn more advanced techniques. Card networks revise their regulations and processes and tools. Your chargeback expert needs to stay up to speed.

Your expert also needs to be focused on both risk mitigation and chargeback representment. You're only going to get satisfactory results and a good return on investment when you're working both ends of the equation.

> **IN THIS CHAPTER**
>
> » Providing good service, free of errors
>
> » Managing recurring payments and shipping issues
>
> » Preventing both criminal and friendly fraud
>
> » Turning to the experts

Chapter **7**

Ten Essential Tips for Preventing Chargebacks

Chargebacks are a costly and dangerous hassle. Although it's important to fight the fight whenever you can, your best bet is to keep chargebacks from happening in the first place. Following are ten areas of focus that can help you steer clear of the trouble that chargebacks can cause.

Connect with Customers

TIP

Make sure your contact information is easy to find. It should be anywhere and everywhere a customer might look — on your website, on your invoice, in your social media activity, on every piece of correspondence you send, whether by mail or email. And be sure to answer the phone quickly. Don't let it ring and ring.

To Err Is Dangerous

Mistakes may happen, but you'll be glad if you can figure out a way to make them happen less frequently. The main thing is to be sure your people are being as vigilant and careful as possible. Establish best practices, offer training, and then get your team to follow them. And be sure they know the card network's rules and procedures.

TIP

For example, don't ever accept an expired card. It's bound to come back to bite you. When a customer asks for a credit or a cancellation, do your best to provide one. If an issuer requests a copy of some sort of information, submit it in a timely manner.

Keep Tabs on Recurring Payments

TIP

Be sure customers know what they're getting. Don't surprise them with a recurring payment plan; be upfront with the terms of service. Consider a contract with no strings attached, and then make it easy for the customer to cancel. When a customer asks to cancel, take care of it promptly. Also, send out a reminder before a recurring payment hits.

Ship Away Those Shipping Problems

Customers feel helpless in that window of time between when they submit an online order and when it arrives. Ideally, that time will be as short as possible, but however long it is, it's best to keep the customer fully informed. Be sure each shipping option clearly spells out the expected delivery time, and make it easy for the customer to track the order and shipping status.

Customers get especially bothered by backorders. If your shipment is going to be delayed because you don't yet have the product in stock, be sure to let the customer know, and offer the chance to cancel the order.

Honesty Is the Best Policy

There's no question that you're running an honest operation. But are your customers getting the full and complete picture of the products or services you're marketing? That isn't always easy to accomplish in the world of card-not-present merchandising, when you're communicating with the customer by way of a website.

Customers need to know exactly what they're buying so they won't be surprised when the package arrives. Product descriptions must be accurate and as detailed as possible. Otherwise you'll end up with chargebacks carrying such reason codes as "not as described" or "services not rendered."

Check Your Toolkit

Criminal fraud may not be the top cause of chargebacks, but it's worth taking every opportunity to prevent bad guys from trying to make fraudulent purchases through your business. The Address Verification Service is an automated service aimed specifically at preventing fraud involving card-not-present transactions. Simply put, it compares the billing address provided by your customer with the one that the issuing bank has on file.

Card security codes also help stop fraud in card-not-present transactions. That three- or four-digit code that's separate from the account number isn't stored anywhere that hackers can access. That means someone buying a stolen card number isn't going to have the code.

TIP

If you do affiliate marketing, you should consider adding affiliate fraud alerts. These special alerts are designed to flag suspicious activities that can arise with affiliate marketing.

Signs of Fraud

Beyond antifraud tools, you have multiple other ways to monitor for potentially fraudulent purchases. Here is a rundown of helpful hints:

- » You always want new customers, but remember that potential fraudsters are likely to be new customers.
- » Fraudsters might be buying a bunch of the same product that they will then resell. They also like to resell big-ticket items.
- » A fraudster may make multiple purchases with different cards, shipped to the same address. Alternatively, the fraudster might make a bunch of purchases with the same card, but with different shipping addresses.
- » If you suspect a purchase is fraudulent, call the cardholder or send a letter to the billing address.

» Get to know your repeat customers, so you can spot suspicious changes in buying habits or shipping addresses that might suggest a fraudulent buyer.

» Use blacklists to weed out known fraudsters, or whitelists to allow only certain customers, such as only buyers from your own country.

Keep Your Data Secure

You want your customers to treat you well by not filing chargebacks. Be sure to treat them well by handling their data with care. To begin with, adhere to the Payment Card Industry Data Security Standard (PCI-DSS). Additional protection measures include tokenization, which puts a third party in charge of card information, and end-to-end encryption, which offers uninterrupted data protection.

More Friendly Fraud Prevention

TIP

Requiring delivery confirmation is a bit of a pain for the customer, but it helps stop friendly fraud. If the customer has confirmed getting your product, he or she is less likely to complain to the bank that it never arrived.

Also, watch out for unusually big purchases, duplicate orders, and incongruities between billing and shipping addresses. Be aware that digital goods are friendly fraud targets, so limit their sale in bulk, and consider setting daily sale limits.

Talk to the Experts

Most of these tips will help you harvest the low-hanging fruit, which is definitely worthwhile, but most types of chargebacks can be reduced only through more intensive management techniques. That's where experts can help.

They help not only because of their expertise, but also because they free your people up to do what you do best: conduct your business. You need to satisfy customers and attract new ones. Let someone else deal with chargebacks.

> **IN THIS CHAPTER**
> » Understanding Mastercard's reason codes
> » Checking the list of Visa reason codes

Appendix
Chargeback Reason Codes

You can't very well dispute a chargeback — or improve a business process — if you don't know what happened. The card networks, when they inform you of a chargeback, include a reason code that explains what the problem is.

Each card networks has its own list of reason codes. This appendix provides the most often-cited codes for the two biggest card networks, Mastercard and Visa.

Reason Codes for Mastercard

If you receive notice of a chargeback involving a Mastercard transaction, it's likely to carry a reason code from this list. Remember, these are the allegations put forth by the customer or the issuing bank — you might have a different version of the story. Here are the most common Mastercard reason codes, as listed at the time of this publication:

> » **4807: Warning Bulletin File.** The issuing bank can't verify that an authorization code was obtained at the time of the transaction.

» **4808: Authorization-Related Chargeback.** The merchant didn't obtain authorization or got it too late.

» **4812: Account Number Not On File.** The issuing bank can't find an account with the number used.

» **4831: Transaction Amount Differs.** The amount the cardholder was charged doesn't match what's on the receipt that the cardholder was given.

» **4834: Point of Interaction Error.** One transaction took place, but it was processed more than once (using the same form of payment, or multiple forms of payment).

» **4837: No Cardholder Authorization.** The cardholder claims he or she did not authorize the transaction.

» **4840: Fraudulent Processing of Transactions.** The merchant is accused of fraudulently processing a transaction (this can happen with duplicate processing).

» **4841: Canceled Recurring or Digital Goods Transactions.** The cardholder wants to stop a recurring charge.

» **4842: Late Presentment.** The charge was not processed in a timely manner (often the account was closed in the meantime).

» **4846: Correct Transaction Currency Code Not Provided.** This may be a dispute in the currency used or a disagreement about a currency conversion.

» **4849: Questionable Merchant Activity.** This transaction violates Mastercard's rules or the merchant was on a Mastercard security list.

» **4850: Installment Billing Dispute.** This is much like 4841, involving recurring charges.

» **4853: Cardholder Dispute.** The wrong item arrived, or it was defective.

» **4854: Cardholder Dispute — Not Elsewhere Classified.** The cardholder claims that a good-faith effort to resolve a dispute didn't turn out well.

» **4855: Goods or Services Not Provided.** The product never arrived, or the service wasn't completed.

» **4859: Addendum, No-Show, or ATM Dispute.** The cardholder claims not to be responsible for a particular transaction.

» **4860: Credit Not Processed.** The cardholder was expecting a credit, and it did not happen.

- **4863: Cardholder Does Not Recognize — Potential Fraud.** The cardholder looked at the statement and couldn't figure out what this transaction was.
- **4870: Chip Liability Shift.** This is a claim involving potential criminal fraud.
- **4871: Chip/PIN Liability Shift.** This also is a suggestion of criminal fraud.

Reason Codes for Visa

Following is a list of the most common chargeback codes identified by Visa, current at the time of publication. Most of them fall into four basic groups. Those starting with 10 are fraud codes, 11 signifies authorization problems, 12 indicates processing errors, and 13 is the signal of a consumer dispute.

- **10.1: EMV Liability Shift Counterfeit Fraud.** The cardholder claims a fraudulent transaction was made, using a counterfeit card.
- **10.2: EMV Liability Shift Non-Counterfeit Fraud.** The cardholder claims this activity was fraudulent, but blames the merchant's EMV terminal.
- **10.3: Other Fraud — Card-Present Environment.** There was actual plastic involved, but it was a fraudulent transaction, according to the cardholder.
- **10.4: Fraud — Card-Absent Environment.** Another transaction not authorized by the cardholder, this time without the card present.
- **10.5: Visa Fraud Monitoring Program.** Visa's Fraud Monitoring Program flagged the transaction, but the issuer didn't provide any additional information.
- **11.1: Card Recovery Bulletin.** The merchant seemingly skipped getting authorization for the transaction.
- **11.2: Declined Authorization.** The authorization was declined, but the charge was pursued and processed anyway.
- **11.3: No Authorization.** Kind of like 11.2, except no one bothered to seek authorization at all, or sought it too late.
- **12.1: Late Presentment.** The charge was not processed in a timely manner.

- **12.2: Incorrect Transaction Code.** The transaction code was wrong (often it went through as a sale when it was supposed to be a credit).
- **12.3: Incorrect Currency.** The currency code was wrong.
- **12.4: Incorrect Account Number.** Someone likely made a typo when entering the account number.
- **12.5: Incorrect Amount.** This might be a math error when figuring out the transaction amount.
- **12.6: Duplicate Processing/Paid by Other Means.** The transaction was processed more than once. In some cases, the transaction happened, but the customer paid in some other way, such as cash or another card.
- **12.7: Invalid Data.** The authorization for the transaction wasn't correct, and/or it wasn't valid.
- **13.1: Merchandise/Services Not Received.** The product never arrived, or the service was not completed.
- **13.2: Canceled Recurring.** The cardholder claims to have canceled a recurring transaction, but was charged anyway.
- **13.3: Not as Described or Defective Merchandise/Services.** The wrong item arrived, or it was defective.
- **13.4: Counterfeit Merchandise.** The merchandise is not what it claims to be.
- **13.5 Misrepresentation.** The cardholder claims a purchased item or service was misrepresented; this is essentially an allegation of false advertising.
- **13.6: Credit Not Processed.** The customer was supposed to receive a credit, but it never got processed.
- **13.7: Cancelled Merchandise/Services.** The cardholder claims to have been charged for an order or service that was cancelled.
- **13.8: Original Credit Transaction Not Accepted.** A voided transaction receipt was not processed; this applies specifically to Europe and inter-regional areas.
- **13.9: Non-Receipt of Cash or Load Transaction Value.** The cardholder used an ATM but didn't receive cash, or only got a partial amount.
- **57: Fraudulent Multiple Transactions.** A charge was sent through more than once, and it shouldn't have been.
- **73: Expired Card.** A charge went through involving an expired card, and no authorization was provided.